SEW MERRY and BRIGHT

21 easy, fun, and festive patterns

Linda Lum DeBono

Martingale®
Create with Confidence

Sew Merry and Bright: 21 Easy, Fun, and Festive Patterns
© 2012 by Linda Lum DeBono

Martingale®
19021 120th Ave. NE, Ste. 102
Bothell, WA 98011-9511 USA
ShopMartingale.com

Printed in China
17 16 15 14 13 12   8 7 6 5 4 3 2 1

Library of Congress Cataloging-in-Publication Data

Library of Congress Control Number: 2012011842
ISBN: 978-1-60468-180-2

Dedication

For my grandmother, Yuet Yau Lin. I consider myself fortunate to have been blessed with her strength and perseverance. It's what drives me in all that I do.

Mission Statement

Dedicated to providing quality products and service to inspire creativity.

Credits
President & CEO: Tom Wierzbicki
Editor in Chief: Mary V. Green
Design Director: Paula Schlosser
Managing Editor: Karen Costello Soltys
Technical Editor: Rebecca Kemp Brent
Copy Editor: Sheila Chapman Ryan
Production Manager: Regina Girard
Illustrator: Adrienne Smitke
Cover Designer: Shelly Garrison
Text Designer: Connor Chin
Photographer: Brent Kane

Contents

Projects

Introduction

While writing the manuscript for this book, I celebrated the 10-year anniversary of the official launch of my quilt-design business. I thought back over the body of work that I'd produced over the past decade. Two things have been constant in my design process—color and celebration. For this reason, I've designed a lot of winter holiday projects: I love the festive colors that define this season.

I have two little boys, Adam and Alex, who love the holidays and who love fun and bright colors just as much as their momma! We've had fun decorating the house in fuchsia, chartreuse, and turquoise one holiday and silver and teal another year. We think that there's no official colorway that you must adhere to in your holiday fabric selections.

I had the pleasure of working with some very fabulous holiday fabrics for the projects in this book. Whether you like to use bright, modern novelty prints or a more traditional palette, I'm sure that you'll enjoy making these projects as much as I enjoyed designing them.

Happy Holidays!
-Linda

How Many More?

Whenever we drive to Toronto to visit family, my older son, Adam, loves to ask us, "How many more miles until we get there?" We always point to the GPS to let him know the exact number of miles remaining. When December rolls around, my little guy, Alex, likes to ask us, "How many more days until Christmas?" He does this many times a day, every day, until Christmas. I think this adorable Advent calendar will keep him on track, don't you?

Designed and made by
Linda Lum DeBono

Finished size: 19" x 37"
(excluding hanging tab)
Finished pocket size: 3" x 3"

Materials

1 ⅛ yards of 36"-wide or ⅔ yard of 72"-wide white wool felt for background

1 ⅛ yards of 36"-wide or ⅔ yard of 72"-wide red wool felt for backing

9" x 12" craft cut or ⅛ yard *each* of a colorful assortment of wool felt for pockets and appliqué

8" x 12" piece of turquoise wool for hanging tab

⅝ yard of 1"-wide fuchsia rickrack for decorative trim

Copy/printer paper for appliqué templates

Masking tape

Cutting

From the white felt, cut:
   1 rectangle, 19" x 37"

From the red felt, cut:
   1 rectangle, 19" x 37"

From the assorted felt, cut:
   24 squares, 3" x 3"
   24 using circle pattern (page 7)

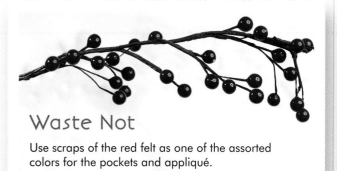

Waste Not

Use scraps of the red felt as one of the assorted colors for the pockets and appliqué.

Directions

Seam allowances are ¼" unless otherwise indicated.

1 Use the patterns to trace the numbers from 1 to 24 onto paper and cut them out. One at a time, hold a number template on top of the desired felt color and, using fine embroidery scissors, carefully cut the number from the felt. Though the cutting is a little tricky, the end result is well worth the effort.

2 Appliqué each number from 1 to 24 onto a contrasting felt circle by sewing a straight stitch along the center of each numeral with matching thread, following the number's shape.

3 Center each circle on a contrasting 3"-square pocket front and machine stitch in place using a zigzag stitch that's 3 mm wide and 2 mm long. Choose thread that matches the circle color and position the stitch so it overcasts the circle edges.

4 Use the masking tape to mark the pocket placements on the white felt background, referring to the illustration at right for details. The pockets in each row are 1" apart; the rows are 2" apart. The side margins are 2" wide and the top margin is 4" high. Measure each distance and adhere masking tape to create a placement

grid; remove the masking tape when all the pockets are in position.

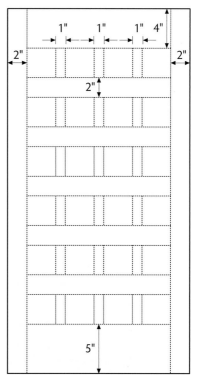

Use 1"-wide masking tape to mark pocket placements on the background fabric.

5 Topstitch the pockets in place with matching thread and a straight stitch ⅛" from the side and bottom edges. Do not sew the top edges.

6 Center the rickrack across the bottom margin, with the points about 2" below the bottom row of pockets. Fold the raw edges of the rickrack to the back of the calendar, pin, and sew with a machine straight stitch through the center of the rickrack.

7 Fold the hanging tab fabric in half lengthwise and pin to the calendar wrong side, centering it between the side edges. The tab's fold should extend outward, with the calendar overlapping the tab's raw edges by ½". Pin the backing to the calendar front, wrong sides together, concealing the tab and rickrack raw edges. Topstitch ¼" from all four outer edges with matching thread to secure the backing and the hanging tab.

8 Each day during the countdown to Christmas, you can fill a pocket with a special treat. Or, start with the treats in place, and let your child select one each day from December 1 through Christmas Eve!

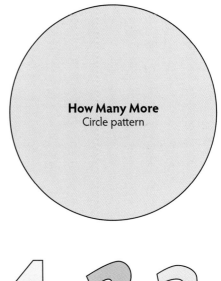

How Many More
Circle pattern

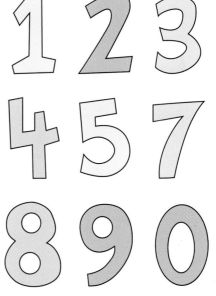

12 Little Birdies

I love little birds. I have pretty bird ornaments of every kind on my Christmas tree. There are glittery ones, fine-feathered ones, and now I can add these lovely wool-felt birds to the collection. This flock of birds will help you count down the last 12 days until Christmas. Tweet! Tweet!

Designed and made by
Linda Lum DeBono

Finished size: 7" x 5¼"

Materials

15 assorted 9" x 12" sheets of wool felt in bright colors

2½ yards of ⅜"-wide green-and-cream gingham ribbon

12 silver seed beads

Beading needle and thread

Polyester fiberfill for stuffing

Cutting

Patterns for bird are on page 59; numbers are on page 7.

From the wool felt, cut:

    12 matching pairs using bird pattern, reversing one in each pair

    12 using wing pattern

From the ribbon, cut:

    12 pieces, 7½" long

Directions

1 Trace the numbers from 1 to 12 onto paper and cut them out. Working on one numeral at a time, hold a number template on top of the desired felt color and carefully cut the number from the felt, using fine embroidery scissors. The cutting is a little tricky, but the end result is well worth the effort.

2 Stitch a number to a contrasting wing with a machine straight stitch through the center of the numeral, following the number's shape.

3 Sew the bottom half of each wing to the right side of a contrasting bird body, referring to the illustration and stitching from A to B using a 3 mm wide and 2 mm long zigzag stitch.

4 Pin a matching pair of bird bodies wrong sides together. Fold a ribbon length in half and slip the ends between the body front and back at the dot, tucking ½" of ribbon between the felt pieces.

5 Starting at the bottom, use a zigzag stitch 3 mm wide and 2 mm long to sew the body front and back together. Position the zigzag stitch to overcast the edges of the felt pieces. Backstitch at the beginning and end to secure and leave a 2" opening along the bottom for stuffing.

6 Stuff the bird through the opening with polyester fiberfill. Pin the felt edges together, moving the filling aside, and finish sewing the dove bodies together. Work the bird between your fingers to distribute the stuffing evenly.

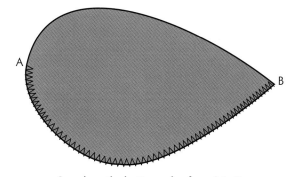

Sew along the bottom edge from A to B.

So Sweet Stocking

Candy-cane printed fabric and spinning yo-yos with fun button centers make this stocking sweet—without the calories!

Designed and made by
Linda Lum DeBono

Finished size: 13" x 23½"

Materials

Yardage is based on 42"-wide fabric.

⅞ yard of green candy-cane print for stocking front and back

¾ yard of red-checked print for ruched stocking cuff and yo-yos

⅞ yard of muslin for stocking-front foundation

⅞ yard of lining fabric

2 pieces of batting, 17" x 28"

12" of 1"-wide black-and-white gingham ribbon

4 green buttons, ⅞" diameter

Right Side Up

The given fabric yardages allow for cutting the stocking front and back lengthwise to take advantage of directional prints.

Assembling the Pattern

Follow one of these methods to assemble the stocking pattern from the full-sized sections on pages 66–70.

Method 1

1. Trace each pattern section onto a piece of pattern paper. Copy, tracing, and wrapping paper are all suitable.
2. Cut out each piece along the lines.
3. Lay the pattern sections side by side, matching the letters (match A to A, B to B, etc.); tape the sections together. The sections should not overlap. For stability, turn the assembled pattern over and tape the joins again from the wrong side.

Method 2

1. Begin with a piece of paper at least 17" x 28". Trace the uppermost section near the upper-right corner of the paper, with the stocking upper edge parallel to the paper edge. Do not cut out.
2. Position the paper over the second section pattern with the G and H edges aligned. Trace the second section.
3. Continue tracing the remaining sections onto the paper, matching each with the preceding section, to assemble the full stocking pattern.

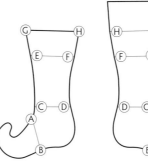

Stocking front

Stocking back, foundation, and lining

Cutting

Patterns for stocking and yo-yos are on pages 66–70. Following the instructions in "Assembling the Pattern" on page 11, join sections 1–5 to make the patterns for the stocking back, foundation, and lining pieces. Remember to reverse the pattern when cutting the stocking back and lining front. Use only sections 1–4 for the stocking-front pattern.

From the green candy-cane print, cut:
    1 using stocking-back pattern
    1 using stocking-front pattern
From the red-checked print, cut:
    1 strip, 4½" x 23"
    4 using yo-yo pattern (page 70)
From the muslin, cut:
    1 using stocking-foundation pattern
From the lining fabric, cut:
    1 using stocking-lining pattern
    1 reversed using stocking-lining pattern

Directions

Seam allowances are ¼" unless otherwise indicated.

1 Make a yo-yo from each red print circle (see "Making Yo-Yos" on page 76). Sew a button to the center of each yo-yo.

2 Sew gathering stitches ¼" from the long top and bottom edges of the red-checked strip. Pin one long edge to the top of the stocking front and pull the gathering stitches gently to fit; stitch. Turn the seam allowances toward the ruched strip and press lightly without flattening the gathers.

3 Lay the assembled front right side up on the foundation. Pin the upper raw edges together and pull the gathering stitches to fit. Sew a scant ¼" from the top edge to stabilize the gathers and baste the ruching to the foundation.

4 Center each stocking piece, right side up, on a batting rectangle. Quilt the layers together with a freehand meandering design or as desired. Trim the batting to match the fabric edges.

5 With right sides together, sew the stocking front to the corresponding lining piece along the upper edge. Be sure the toes on both pieces are pointing in the same direction. Repeat to sew the stocking back to its lining.

6 Open each half of the stocking so it lies flat and press the seams open. Pin the stocking front/lining unit to the stocking back/lining unit along all the raw edges, matching the two lining pieces and the two stocking pieces. Sew around the perimeter, leaving a 3" opening for turning along a straight edge of the lining.

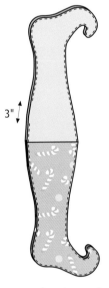

3"

Sew around perimeter, leaving a
3" gap on one side of the lining.

7 Clip around the curves and turn the stocking right side out. Close the gap in the seam allowance by hand or machine. Tuck the lining into the stocking.

8 Topstitch ¼" from the upper edge of the stocking.

9 Fold the ribbon in half and tie the ends into a knot about 3½" from the center fold. Trim the ribbon ends at an angle about 1" beyond the knot. Sew the ribbon fold to the top of the stocking at the heel edge to form a hanging loop. Sew the yo-yos and buttons to the stocking front.

Rudolph's Favorite Stocking

I'm sure that red is Rudolph's favorite color in the whole world. This stocking is perfect for such a hard-working reindeer. I don't think he could resist the reindeer fabric either.

Designed and made by
Linda Lum DeBono

Finished size: 12½" x 21½"
(including ruffle)

Materials

Yardage is based on 42"-wide fabric unless otherwise specified.

4 fat quarters (18" x 22") of red holiday prints for the stocking front

¾ yard of green print for stocking back

½ yard of lining fabric (see "Fabric Saver," below)

¼ yard of black-and-white print for ruffle

2 pieces of batting, 17" x 23"

12" of 1"-wide black-and-white gingham ribbon

Hand-sewing needle

Fabric Saver

Choose a nondirectional print for the lining and cut the lining pieces on the crosswise grain to use less fabric.

Cutting

Patterns for stocking are on pages 67–70.

Following the directions in "Assembling the Pattern" on page 11, join pattern sections 1–4 to make a complete stocking pattern.

From the red fat quarters, cut:
   3 different rectangles, 4½" x 14"
   1 rectangle, 8½" x 14"

From the green print, cut:
   1 reversed using stocking-front pattern

From the lining fabric, cut:
   1 using stocking pattern
   1 reversed using stocking pattern

From the black-and-white fabric, cut:
   1 strip, 5" x 24"

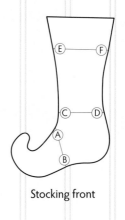

Stocking front

Directions

Seam allowances are ¼" unless otherwise indicated.

1 Sew the 4½" red-print strips together along their long edges. Sew the 8½" red-print strip to the bottom of the strip set. Cut the stocking front from the assembled fabric panel.

2 Place the stocking front right side up on one batting piece and machine quilt with parallel horizontal lines 2" apart, or as desired. Trim the batting to match the stocking edges. Repeat for the stocking back.

3 With right sides together, sew the stocking front to the green-print stocking back. Leave the top edge open.

4 Sew the short ends of the black-and-white strip together to form a tube. Fold the ruffle in half lengthwise, with wrong sides together, and press.

5 Use a sewing needle and thread or long machine stitches to sew a row of basting stitches along the raw edge of the ruffle, through both fabric thicknesses. Pin the ruffle to the stocking, right sides together along the top edge, with the ruffle seam at the stocking's heel seamline. Pull the stitches gently to gather the ruffle to fit the stocking top and pin, distributing the gathers evenly. Baste using a scant ¼" seam allowance.

6 With right sides together, sew the lining pieces together. Leave the top edge open and leave a 3" opening in one lining side seam. Turn the lining right side out and the stocking wrong side out. Place the lining inside the stocking with right sides together. Match the top edges, with the ruffle between the stocking and lining, and pin.

7 Sew all of the layers together along the open top edge. Clip the curves, and then turn the lining and stocking right side out through the opening in the lining seam. Smooth the ruffle away from the stocking and press. Sew the opening closed and tuck the lining into the stocking.

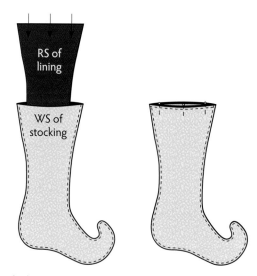

Slip lining inside stocking.   Sew all layers together along the top edge.

8 Topstitch the stocking ¼" below the ruffle seam.

9 Fold the ribbon in half and tie the ends into a knot about 3½" from the center fold. Trim the ribbon ends at an angle about 1" beyond the knot. Sew the ribbon fold to the top of the stocking at the heel edge to form a hanging loop.

Rickrack Rainbow Stocking

Sometimes all it takes is a yard of rickrack to inspire a project. I found this lovely pleated rickrack in Tinsel Trading in New York City one day. I didn't know what to do with it when I bought the rickrack, but I knew that I wanted a yard each in green, red, and fuchsia.

Designed and made by
Linda Lum DeBono

Finished size: 12½" x 23"

Materials

Yardage is based on 42"-wide fabric.

¾ yard of tree print

½ yard of lining fabric (see "Fabric Wise," below)

2 pieces of batting, 17" x 27"

1 yard of 1½"-wide pleated or plain rickrack

10 felt balls, 1" diameter

12" of 1"-wide black-and-white gingham ribbon

Fabric Wise

To save fabric, choose a nondirectional print for the lining and cut the lining pieces on the crosswise grain.

Cutting

Patterns for stocking are on pages 71–74.

Following the directions in "Assembling the Pattern" on page 11, join pattern sections 1–4 to make a complete stocking pattern.

From the tree print, cut:
   1 using stocking pattern
   1 reversed using stocking pattern

From the lining fabric, cut:
   1 using stocking pattern
   1 reversed using stocking pattern

Directions

Seam allowances are ¼" unless otherwise indicated.

1 Center the stocking front right side up on one piece of batting. Pin the layers to secure, and then machine quilt as desired. The sample stocking is quilted with looping freehand lines. Trim the batting to match the stocking piece. Repeat for the stocking back.

2 Measure and mark a line 3¾" below the top of the stocking front. Measure and mark a second line 5" below the first and a third line 5" below the second.

3 Center the rickrack along the first line and sew it to the stocking with a straight machine stitch through the center of the rickrack. Trim the rickrack ends to match the stocking edges. Repeat to sew rickrack to the other two lines.

4 With right sides together, sew the stocking front to the lining front along the top edge. Press the seam open. Repeat to join the stocking and lining backs.

5 With right sides together, sew the stocking/lining front unit to the stocking/lining back unit around all the outer edges. Leave a 3" opening for turning along the straightest part of the lining. Clip the curves and turn the stocking right side out through the gap in the seam. Sew the opening closed by hand or machine.

An Ounce of Protection

Wear a thimble to protect your fingers and provide a helpful push to the needle as you sew through the thick felt balls.

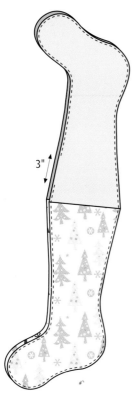

3"

Sew around perimeter, leaving a 3" gap on one side of the lining.

6 Tuck the lining inside the stocking. Press the top edge and topstitch ¼" from the upper edge.

7 Hand stitch the felted balls individually in place along the upper edge of the stocking front, positioning them as shown in the photo. Use doubled thread and a long needle to sew through each ball, taking a bite of felt large enough to hold the balls securely.

8 Fold the ribbon in half and tie the ends into a knot about 3½" from the center fold. Trim the ribbon ends at an angle about 1" beyond the knot. Sew the ribbon fold to the top of the stocking at the heel edge to form a hanging loop.

Star Light, Star Bright Tree Skirt

There's no rule that says stars can only twinkle at the top of a Christmas tree! This twinkling tree skirt will shine at the base of your tree and add some bright color to your room.

Designed and made by
Linda Lum DeBono

Finished size: 48½" x 48½"

Materials

Yardage is based on 42"-wide fabric.

⅞ yard of black snowflake print for star blocks and binding

¾ yard of candy-cane print for tree-skirt center

½ yard of red star print for tree-skirt corners

½ yard of red elf print for Star-block centers

½ yard of white novelty print for Star blocks

¼ yard of red snowflake print for Star blocks

¼ yard of green print for Star blocks

1¾ yards of fabric for backing

55" x 55" batting square

1 package store-bought, double-fold ½"-wide bias binding

Optional: Thangles foundations for 3" finished half-square
   triangles

Cutting

From the black snowflake print, cut:
   32 squares, 3⅞" x 3⅞"; cut once diagonally to yield
      64 triangles
   5 strips, 2½" x width of fabric

From the candy-cane print, cut:
   1 square, 24½" x 24½"

From the red star print, cut:
   2 squares, 12½" x 12½"; cut once diagonally to yield
   4 triangles

From the red elf print, cut:
   8 squares, 6½" x 6½"

From the white novelty print, cut:
   32 squares, 3⅞" x 3⅞"; cut once diagonally to yield
      64 triangles

From the red snowflake print, cut:
   16 squares, 3⅞" x 3⅞"; cut once diagonally to yield
      32 triangles

From the green print, cut:
   16 squares, 3⅞" x 3⅞"; cut once diagonally to yield
      32 triangles

Shortcut to Precision Piecing

If you prefer, use Thangles printed foundations to make the half-square triangles for the
Star blocks. Substitute the cutting directions below and use the assembly directions on the
Thangles package to make the units described in step 1.

From the black snowflake print, cut:
   16 rectangles, 3½" x 9¼"

From the red snowflake print, cut:
   8 rectangles, 3½" x 9¼"

From the white novelty print, cut:
   16 rectangles, 3½" x 9¼"

From the green print, cut:
   8 rectangles, 3½" x 9¼"

Directions

Seam allowances are ¼" unless otherwise indicated.

1 Sew each black triangle to a white triangle to make 64 half-square-triangle units. Sew each red snowflake print triangle to a green triangle to make 32 units.

2 Arrange the black/white units in pairs as shown. Sew each pair together to create a star-peak unit. Make 32.

Make 32.

3 Sew star-peak units to two opposite sides of each elf-print center square. Make eight.

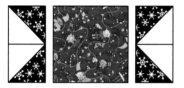

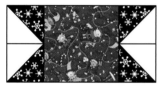

Make 8.

4 Stitch a red/green half-square-triangle unit to each end of the remaining star-peak units. Position the green fabric next to the black fabric at each seam. Make 16 rows.

Make 16.

5 Sew the step 4 rows to the top and bottom of each unit from step 3 to complete the Star blocks. Make eight.

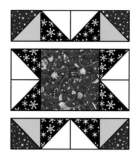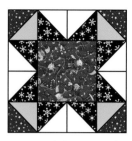

Make 8.

6 Join the star blocks into four pairs.

7 Sew a red star triangle to each side of a block pair. Make two. These are the top and bottom rows of the tree skirt.

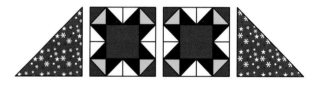

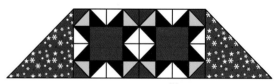

Tree skirt top and bottom.
Make 2.

8 Stitch a pair of blocks to each side of the candy-
cane square to make the center row of the tree
skirt. Join the top and bottom rows to the center row to
complete the tree-skirt top.

9 Layer the tree-skirt top, batting and backing.
Baste the layers together and quilt with loopy, meandering lines or as desired.

10 Draw a 6½" diameter circle on plain paper and
cut out. Fold the template and tree skirt in half
twice to find the center points. Pin the template to the tree
skirt, matching the centers.

11 Cut along the seamline between two star blocks
and continue cutting in a straight line until you
reach the edge of the circle. Cut around the outer edge
of the circle template. Unpin and remove the template.

12 Remove the selvages from the black-print strips
and join them to create a continuous length.
Press the strip in half lengthwise, wrong sides together,
and bind the straight edges of the tree skirt, beginning
and ending at the center opening and mitering the corners (see "Straight-Grain Binding" on page 77).

13 Open the folds in the purchased bias tape and
press ¼" to the wrong side at the end. Match one
long raw edge of the bias tape to the edge of the center
opening, right sides together, and pin, easing the bias
tape around the curve. Cut the excess tape ¼" beyond
the end of the circle, press the ¼" to the wrong side, and
finish pinning.

14 Sew the bias tape to the tree skirt along the
crease, ¼" from the tape's edge. Refold the bias
tape, enclosing the raw edges, and slip-stitch the tape to
the skirt wrong side along the curved seamline. Topstitch
the finished binding ¼" from the folded edge.

Noel Pillow

The zig and zag of the chevron background pattern add a bit of modern funk and movement to what could be just an ordinary pillow. You can choose alternating strips of white and a single color as I did, or go wild by creating strips of mixed colors, patterns, and prints.

Designed and made by Linda Lum DeBono

Finished size: 18" x 12"

Materials

Yardage is based on 42"-wide fabric unless otherwise specified.

¼ yard of apple-green print for background

¼ yard of white fabric for background

Fat quarter of red print for appliqué

½ yard of fabric for backing

21" x 15" piece of batting

9" x 12" piece of fusible web

10" x 13" piece of tear-away stabilizer (see "Stabilizer" on page 75)

Polyester fiberfill

Optional: Thangles foundations for 3" finished half-square triangles (see "Shortcut to Precision Piecing" on page 20)

Cutting

Appliqué patterns are on page 62.

From the apple-green print, cut:
   12 squares, 3⅞" x 3⅞"; cut once diagonally to yield 24 triangles

From the white fabric, cut:
   12 squares, 3⅞" x 3⅞"; cut once diagonally to yield 24 triangles

From the backing fabric, cut:
   1 rectangle, 12½" x 18½"

Thangles Cutting Instructions

If using the optional Thangles foundation papers, substitute these cutting instructions.

From the apple-green print, cut:
   6 rectangles, 3½" x 9¼"

From the white fabric, cut:
   6 rectangles, 3½" x 9¼"

Directions

Seam allowances are ¼" unless otherwise indicated.

1 Sew each green triangle to a white triangle to make 24 half-square-triangle units.

2 Arrange the half-square-triangle units into four rows of six, forming a zigzag pattern. Sew the blocks together in rows, and then join the rows to complete the background for the pillow top.

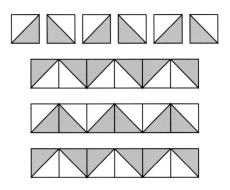

3 Trace the letters on page 62 onto the paper side of the fusible web. Following the manufacturer's instructions, fuse the web to the wrong side of the red fabric. Cut out each letter. Remove the paper backing and fuse the letters to the pieced pillow top, referring to the photo for placement (see "Fusible Machine Appliqué" on page 76).

4 Pin the stabilizer underneath the pieced pillow front. Using a zigzag stitch that's 3 mm wide and 2 mm long and red thread, stitch the letters to the pieced pillow front. Position the stitch so it overcasts the raw edges of the letters. Tear away the excess stabilizer.

5 Center the pieced front right side up on the batting rectangle. Stitch in the ditch and along the letter edges to quilt the layers together. Add a line of quilting along the center of each white zigzag, echoing the shape of the piecing. Trim the batting to match the pillow top.

6 With right sides together, sew the pillow front to the pillow back. Leave a 5" opening for turning along the bottom edge. Clip the corners diagonally to reduce bulk and turn the pillow right side out. Use a point turner or other tool to work the corners into position. Press the pillow, folding the seam allowances to the wrong side along the opening.

7 Stuff the pillow with polyester fiberfill and slip-stitch the opening closed.

Peace Place Mat

I fell in love with this fun print and thought that it was busy enough to stand alone, with very little piecing. A simple word appliquéd to the place mat adds a whimsical finishing touch.

Designed and made by
Linda Lum DeBono

Finished size: 18" x 14"

Materials

Yardage is based on 42"-wide fabric unless otherwise specified.

Fat quarter of turquoise novelty print for place-mat front

Fat quarter of red tone-on-tone print for appliqué background

Fat quarter of green fabric for backing

Fat quarter or 9" x 12" scrap of diamond-print fabric for *Peace* appliqué

9" x 12" piece of fusible web

6½" x 18½" rectangle of tear-away stabilizer (see "Stabilizer" on page 75)

Directions

Seam allowances are ¼" unless otherwise indicated.

1 Trace the letters on page 64 onto fusible web. Be sure to trace two e shapes. Following the manufacturer's instructions, iron the fusible web to the wrong side of the diamond-print fabric and cut out the letters (see "Fusible Machine Appliqué" on page 76).

2 Remove the paper and arrange the letters on the red rectangle, centering the word from side to side and placing the letters 1½" above the raw edge. Fuse the letters to the fabric. Place a layer of stabilizer underneath the fabric. Use a zigzag stitch that's 3 mm wide and 2 mm long and turquoise thread to stitch around the letters, overcasting the raw edges.

3 With right sides together, sew the turquoise-print rectangles to the top and bottom of the appliquéd rectangle. If using a directional print, be sure all the images are upright.

Cutting

Appliqué patterns are on page 64.

From the turquoise novelty print, cut:
2 rectangles, 4½" x 18½"

From the red print, cut:
1 rectangle, 6½" x 18½"

From the green fabric, cut:
1 rectangle, 14½" x 18½"

Top of the Class

When using directional prints for the place mat, position the print perpendicular to the 18½" edges so the words and images will be correctly oriented in the finished project.

4 With right sides together, pin and sew the pieced place-mat front to the green rectangle. Leave a 5" opening along the bottom edge for turning. Clip the corners diagonally to reduce bulk and turn the project right side out. Use a point turner or other tool to ease the fabric into nice, sharp corners. Press carefully, turning the seam allowances along the gap to the wrong side, and slip-stitch the opening closed.

5 Topstitch ¼" from the outer edges of the rectangle.

Joy Place Mat

Oh, joy! This place mat is so happy and bright. You can easily swap out the fabrics and add your own touch to the look of the design.

Designed and made by
Linda Lum DeBono

Finished size: 18" x 14"

Materials

Yardage is based on 42"-wide fabric unless otherwise specified.

Fat quarter of red print for appliqué background

Fat quarter of green novelty print for place mat

Fat quarter of green fabric for backing

9" square of multicolor-striped fabric for place mat

9" x 6" rectangle of diamond print for appliqué letters

9" x 6" square of fusible web

8½" x 11½" rectangle of tear-away stabilizer

   (see "Stabilizer" on page 75)

Thread Color

Select a thread for appliqué that matches the darkest color in the appliqué fabric to maximize coverage over the raw edges.

Cutting

Appliqué patterns are on page 65.

From the red print, cut:
   1 rectangle, 8½" x 11½"

From the multicolor-striped fabric, cut:
   1 rectangle, 7½" x 8½", with stripes parallel to the 8½" sides

From the green novelty print, cut:
   1 rectangle, 6½" x 18½", with directional print running parallel to the 6½" sides

From the green fabric, cut:
   1 rectangle, 14½" x 18½"

Directions

Seam allowances are ¼" unless otherwise indicated.

1 Trace the letters on page 65 onto fusible web. Following the manufacturer's instructions, iron the fusible web to the wrong side of the diamond-print fabric and cut out the letters (see "Fusible Machine Appliqué" on page 76).

2 Remove the paper and arrange the letters on the red rectangle, centering the word from side to side. Position the top of the J 1¾" below the upper edge of the rectangle and the base of the o 3¼" above the lower edge of the fabric. Place a layer of stabilizer underneath the fabric. Using turquoise thread, sew a machine zigzag stitch that's 3 mm wide and 2 mm long around the letters, overcasting the raw edges. Tear away the excess stabilizer.

3 Sew the striped rectangle to the left edge of the red rectangle.

4 Sew the green novelty print rectangle to the bottom of the unit.

5 With right sides together, pin and sew the assembled place-mat front to the green rectangle. Leave a 5" opening along the bottom edge for turning. Clip the corners diagonally to reduce bulk and turn the place mat right side out, using a point turner or other tool to shape the corners. Press the place mat carefully, turning the seam allowances along the gap to the wrong side, and slip-stitch the opening closed.

6 Topstitch ¼" from the outer edges of the place mat.

Peace and Joy Runner

This runner is one of the simplest to make yet also the easiest to dress up with fanciful fabrics. I love these fun novelty fabrics in green, aqua, and red. They're all busy fabrics, but they go so well together.

Designed and made by
Linda Lum DeBono

Finished size: 18" x 46"

Materials

Yardage is based on 42"-wide fabric unless otherwise specified.

Fat quarter of red print for appliqué background.

Fat quarter of turquoise novelty print for runner front

Fat quarter of green novelty print for runner front

Fat quarter of red snowflake print for runner front

9" x 12" rectangle of diamond print for appliqué letters

1⅜ yards of fabric for backing

9" x 12" rectangle of fusible web

Two 8½" x 18½" pieces of tear-away stabilizer

(see "Stabilizer" on page 75)

Cutting

From the red print, cut:
2 rectangles, 8½" x 18½"

From the turquoise novelty print, cut:
2 rectangles, 4" x 18½"

From the green novelty print, cut:
2 rectangles, 4½" x 18½"

From the snowflake print, cut:
1 rectangle, 15" x 18½"

From the backing fabric, cut:
1 rectangle, 18½" x 46½"

Directions

Seam allowances are ¼" unless otherwise indicated.

1 Trace the *Peace* and *Joy* letters (pages 64 and 65) onto fusible web. Be sure to trace two e pieces. Iron the fusible web to the wrong side of the diamond-print fabric and cut out each letter (see "Fusible Machine Appliqué" on page 76).

2 Center each word on one of the red rectangles and fuse. Place a piece of stabilizer underneath the fabric. Thread your needle with coordinating thread, set the machine for a zigzag stitch that's 3 mm wide and 2 mm long, and stitch around the perimeter of each letter. Position the stitches to overcast the appliqué edges for a clean finish. Tear away the excess stabilizer.

3 Sew the rectangles together as shown. Consider the directions of the dimensional prints, if used. Notice that the fabric order is different on each end of the runner.

4 With right sides together, pin and sew the assembled runner to the backing rectangle, leaving a 5" opening near the center of one long side for turning. Clip the corners diagonally to reduce bulk and turn the runner right side out. Use a point turner or other tool to shape the sharp corners. Press the entire runner, turning the seam allowances along the gap to the wrong side.

5 Slip-stitch the opening closed. Topstitch ¼" from the outer edges of the table runner.

Heads Up!

If the novelty prints are directional—that is, they have a definite "up" direction—cut the runner pieces so the print is parallel to the short sides of the rectangles. Then, when piecing, arrange the rectangles so the *top* of each directional print lies toward the center of the runner. The print will be right side up when the ends of the runner hang off the table.

Happy Jolly Place Mat

I fell in love with the happy jolliness of the large tree print. The colors and the whimsy of the print just scream, "Let's have some fun!"

Designed and made by
Linda Lum DeBono

Finished size: 18" x 12"

Materials

Yardage is based on 42"-wide fabric unless otherwise specified.

Fat quarter of tree print for place-mat front

6" x 8" rectangle *each* of 3 red-and-white prints for place-mat front

Fat quarter of black-and-white print for place-mat front

Fat quarter of fabric for backing

Top Tip

When using directional prints, be sure all will be correctly oriented in the finished place mat.

Cutting

From the tree print, cut:
1 square, 12½" x 12½"

From *each of two* red-and-white prints, cut:
1 rectangle, 5" x 6½" (2 total)

From the third red-and-white print, cut:
1 rectangle, 3½" x 6½"

From the black-and-white print, cut:
1 strip, 2½" x 12½"

From backing fabric, cut:
1 rectangle, 12½" x 18½"

Directions

Seam allowances are ¼" unless otherwise indicated.

1 Sew the three red-print rectangles together along their long edges, placing the smaller rectangle between the larger ones.

2 Fold the black-and-white strip in half lengthwise, wrong sides together, and press. Lay the folded strip on the right edge of the tree-print square, matching the raw edges, and pin.

3 Lay the assembled red prints on the tree-print square, right sides together, covering the folded strip. Match the raw edges and sew all the layers together. Open the seam and press the black-and-white print toward the red prints, pressing the seam allowances toward the tree-print square. Topstitch the tree print square ¼" from the seam.

4 With right sides together, sew the assembled place-mat front and the backing rectangle together. Leave a 5" opening along the bottom edge for turning. Clip the corners diagonally to reduce bulk and turn the place mat right side out.

5 Use a point turner or other tool to smooth the corners into shape. Press the place mat, turning the raw edges to the wrong side along the opening, and slip-stitch the opening closed.

6 Topstitch ¼" from the outside edges of the place mat.

Topstitch.

It's a Green Christmas!
Place Mat

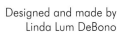hough made in traditional
Christmas colors, this place
mat is still funky and modern!
Add depth by using different
shades of the same color.

Designed and made by
Linda Lum DeBono

Finished size: 18" x 12"

Materials

Yardage is based on 42"-wide fabric unless otherwise specified.

1 fat quarter *each* of green reindeer print, green snow-flake print, white tree print, and diamond print for place-mat front

1 fat quarter for place-mat back

Directional Prints

If you choose directional prints for the project, cut the place-mat rectangles with the design parallel to the 12½" edges.

Cutting

From the green reindeer print, cut:
1 rectangle, 7½"x 12½"

From the green snowflake print, cut:
1 rectangle, 4½"x 12½"

From the white tree print, cut:
1 rectangle, 7½"x 12½"

From the diamond print, cut:
2 strips, 2½"x 12½"

From the backing fabric, cut:
1 rectangle, 12½"x 18½"

Directions

Seam allowances are ¼" unless otherwise indicated.

1 Fold each diamond-print strip in half lengthwise, wrong sides together, and press. Lay one folded strip along each long edge of the green snowflake rectangle, right sides together and matching the raw edges; pin.

2 Pin the reindeer-print rectangle to the left edge of the snowflake rectangle, right sides together and with the folded strip between the fabrics. Sew and press the seam allowances toward the snowflake rectangle; press the diamond strip toward the reindeer print on the right side. Topstitch the snowflake print ¼" from the seam.

3 Pin the tree print to the right edge of the snowflake section, right sides together and with the folded strip between the fabrics. Sew and press the seam allowances toward the snowflake rectangle; press the diamond strip toward the tree print on the right side.

4 Topstitch the snowflake print ¼" from the seam.

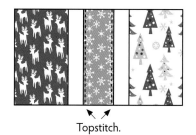

Topstitch.

5 With right sides together, sew the place-mat front to the place-mat back. Leave a 5" opening for turning along the bottom edge. Clip the corners diagonally to reduce bulk and turn the place mat right side out.

6 Use a point turner or other tool to gently work the corners into place. Press the place mat, turning the raw edges to the wrong side along the opening, and slip-stitch the opening closed.

7 Topstitch ¼" from the outer edges of the place mat.

Holly Jolly Runner

I couldn't get enough of these adorable reindeer! The fabric with the white background gives the whole runner a burst of fun, and the black-and-white polka dots, as always, add a lot of whimsy.

Designed and made by
Linda Lum DeBono

Finished size: 12" x 40"

Materials

Yardage is based on 42"-wide fabric unless otherwise specified.

Fat quarter of green tree print

Fat quarter of green snowflake print

Fat quarter of green reindeer print

Fat quarter of red tree print

Fat quarter of red reindeer print

Fat quarter of white holiday print

Fat quarter of red snowflake print

¼ yard of black-and-white print

½ yard of fabric for backing

Cutting

From the green tree print, cut:
1 rectangle, 7½" x 12½"

From the green snowflake print, cut:
1 rectangle, 7½" x 12½"

From the green reindeer print, cut:
1 rectangle, 7½" x 12½"

From the red tree print, cut:
1 rectangle, 4½" x 12½"

From the red reindeer print, cut:
1 rectangle, 4½" x 12½"

From the red snowflake print, cut:
1 rectangle, 4½" x 12½"

From the white holiday print, cut:
1 rectangle, 7½" x 12½"

From the black-and-white print, cut:
6 strips, 2½" x 12½"

From the backing fabric, cut:
1 rectangle, 12½" x 40½"

Everything Upright

Be aware of directional prints as you cut the pieces. In the sample, all the prints are cut parallel to the 12½" edges. For a different look, cut the prints parallel to the shorter edges of each rectangle and arrange them with their tops toward the center of the runner, like in the "Peace and Joy Runner" on page 30.

Directions

Seam allowances are ¼" unless otherwise indicated.

1 Fold and press each black-and-white strip in half lengthwise with the wrong sides together.

2 Place a pressed strip along each long edge of all three red rectangles, right sides together and matching the raw edges; pin.

3 Sew the green-print and white-print rectangles to the red-print rectangles as shown, securing the black-and-white strips between the rectangles.

4 Press each seam toward the red rectangle, pressing the black-and-white strips away from the red rectangles. Topstitch each red rectangle ¼" away from each seam.

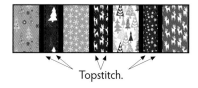

Topstitch.

5 With right sides together, sew the assembled runner front to the backing fabric. Leave a 5" opening for turning near the center of one long side. Clip the corners diagonally to reduce bulk and turn the runner right side out.

6 Gently work the corners into position, making sharp angles. Use a point turner or other tool to assist. Press the runner, turning the raw edges to the wrong side along the opening, and slip-stitch the opening closed.

7 Topstitch ¼" from the outer edges of the runner.

Lovey-Dovey

Doves are a symbol of love and peace. Hang this ornament on your Christmas tree or anywhere you want to share that beautiful message.

Designed and made by
Linda Lum DeBono

Finished size: 6¾" x 5"

Materials

8" x 12" piece of blue wool felt

3" x 3" square of red wool felt

Assorted green seed beads, oval beads, and pearls

Beading thread

Beading needle

Polyester fiberfill

Cutting

Patterns for the dove body and heart are on page 61.

From the blue wool felt, cut:
   1 using dove pattern
   1 reversed using dove pattern

From the red wool felt, cut:
   1 using heart pattern

Directions

1 Using the photograph as a guide, pin the heart to the front of the dove. Use a zigzag stitch that's 3 mm wide and 2 mm long and matching thread to sew the heart to the front of the body, positioning the stitch so it overcasts the heart edges.

2 Layer and pin the dove bodies, wrong sides together. Change to thread that matches the dove body and sew the bodies together with the zigzag settings from step 1. Begin sewing on the bottom edge of the body near the base of the tail and sew around the body until an opening of 2" to 3" remains, positioning the stitch to overcast the body edges.

3 Lightly stuff the dove body with fiberfill. Pin the bodies together at the opening, matching the raw edges and pushing the stuffing aside. Finish sewing the body together, closing the gap. Massage the stuffing back into position.

4 Thread a beading needle with a double strand of beading thread. Bring the thread to the right side on the upper edge of the dove as indicated on the pattern, burying the knot inside the ornament, and take a few backstitches in place to secure. String assorted beads to make a 7" length. Fasten off the thread securely at the same spot where the loop began, burying the thread ends inside the ornament.

5 Sew a single seed bead to the dove's head for the eye, referring to the pattern for placement.

Wonky Tree

I like to select Christmas trees that are a bit wonky. If it's got character, that's the one I want.

Designed and made by
Linda Lum DeBono

Finished size: 6" x 8"

Materials

8" x 10" piece of green wool felt

1½" x 2" piece of brown wool felt

Assorted blue and green seed beads

Beading thread

Beading needle

Polyester fiberfill

Cutting

Patterns for the tree are on page 61.

From the green wool felt, cut:
  1 using tree pattern
  1 reversed using tree pattern

From the brown wool felt, cut:
  1 using trunk pattern
  1 reversed using trunk pattern

Directions

1 Set the machine for a zigzag stitch that's 3 mm wide and 2 mm long. With matching thread, sew the trunk sides and bottom edges together. Position the zigzag stitches to overcast the felt edges and leave the top of the trunk open. Pin the trunk to the wrong side of one tree body, centering it along the bottom edge with the tree body overlapping the trunk ¼".

2 Layer the tree bodies with wrong sides together, matching the raw edges and with the upper edge of the tree trunk between the felt layers. Using the zigzag stitch from step 1, sew the trees together with a zigzag stitch and matching thread. Begin by sewing across the trunk through all layers, and then continue around the tree until only 2" to 3" remain unsewn.

3 Stuff the tree lightly with fiberfill. Finish sewing the remainder of the tree outline, closing the opening.

4 Thread a beading needle with a double strand of beading thread. Bring the thread to the right side at the top point of the tree, burying the knot inside the ornament, and take a few backstitches in place to secure. String assorted beads to make a 7" length. Fasten off the thread securely at the same spot where the loop began, burying the thread ends inside the ornament.

Oh Nuts!

My little guy Alex loves critters of all sorts, and one of his favorite ornaments is a glittery glass squirrel. I thought that this wool one would make a fun addition to his collection.

Designed and made by
Linda Lum DeBono

Finished size: 5" x 6"

Materials

8" x 12" piece of brown wool felt

Assorted blue and green seed beads

1 seed bead for eye

White embroidery floss

Embroidery needle

Beading thread

Beading needle

Polyester fiberfill

Cutting

Pattern for the squirrel is on page 59.

From the brown felt, cut:

1 using squirrel pattern

1 reversed using squirrel pattern

Directions

1 Transfer the embroidery lines from the pattern to the front of the squirrel.

2 Embroider each line with a backstitch and two strands of embroidery floss.

3 Pin the two bodies with wrong sides together. Set the machine for a zigzag stitch that's 3 mm wide and 2 mm long and sew the pieces together, leaving a 2" gap in the seam for stuffing. Use matching thread and position the stitch to overcast the felt edges.

4 Lightly stuff the squirrel with fiberfill. Pin the opening closed, pushing the fiberfill out of the way, and complete the seam around the squirrel body. Massage the squirrel to redistribute the fiberfill evenly.

5 Thread a beading needle with a double strand of beading thread. Bring the needle to the right side of the tail as indicated on the pattern piece, burying the knot inside the ornament, and take several small stitches to secure the thread. String 7" of seed beads onto the beading thread, and then fasten the thread to the squirrel at the mark to form a hanging loop. Bury the thread tails between the fabric layers.

6 With beading thread and needle, sew a single bead for the eye at the location marked on the pattern.

Transferring Embroidery Designs

Transferring embroidery placement lines can be a bit tricky when working with dark-colored felt. Here's the method that I used when making my squirrel:

1. Cut the paper template along the embroidery lines on the tail and body.
2. Pin the template to the front wool-felt body.
3. Use a marking pencil to draw the embroidery lines on the felt by lifting the paper template along one cut line at a time. Follow the curved line, tracing along the edge of the template.

Matryoshka Love

When I was a little girl, a family friend gave me a set of *matryoshka* dolls, also known as Russian nesting dolls. Oh, how I loved them. I was mesmerized by how the little dolls fit so well into each other. It was like magic. I still have the set of dolls and they are still magical.

Designed and made by
Linda Lum DeBono

Finished sizes: 4" x 5½"
2½" x 3½"
1½" x 2¼"

Materials

9" x 12" pieces (craft cut size) of wool felt in the following colors: beige, brown, red, green, and turquoise

7" length of ¾"-wide green scalloped lace

Assorted blue and green seed beads

Brown embroidery floss

Beading thread

Beading needle

Cutting

Patterns for the dolls are on page 60.

From the beige wool felt, cut:
1 using large face pattern
1 using medium face pattern
1 using small face pattern

From the brown wool felt, cut:
1 using large hair pattern
1 using medium hair pattern
1 using small hair pattern

From the red wool felt, cut:
1 using large scarf pattern
1 using medium scarf pattern
1 using small body pattern

From the green wool felt, cut:
1 using large body pattern
1 using large pocket pattern
1 using small scarf pattern

From the turquoise wool felt, cut:
1 using medium body pattern
1 using medium pocket pattern

Directions

Large Matryoshka

1 Embroider the eyes and mouth with three strands of embroidery floss. Use French knots for the eyes, straight stitches for the lashes, and an outline stitch for the eyelids and mouth.

2 Using a zigzag stitch that's 2 mm wide and 0.5 mm long and matching thread, sew the face and the hair to the scarf. Position the stitch so it overcasts the edges of the appliquéd shapes.

3 Appliqué the scarf to the body with matching thread and the stitch from step 2.

4 Lay the lace on the pocket right side, ¾" below the upper edge of the pocket and allowing ½" of lace to extend beyond the pocket edges. Sew the lace to the pocket front using a satin-length zigzag stitch (2 mm wide and 0.3 to 0.4 mm long) to overcast the lace header to the pocket.

5 Position the pocket on the body, right sides up and matching the raw edges. Tuck the ends of the lace between the pocket and the body. Edgestitch the pocket to the body along the outer edges, leaving the top of the pocket open and securing the lace ends.

6 Thread the beading needle with a double strand of beading thread. Secure the thread at the top of the matryoshka's head, hiding the knot between fabric layers. String 7" of beads onto the thread. Fasten the thread end beside the beginning point, forming a hanging loop.

Small and Medium Matryoshkas

Repeat the steps for the large matryoshka, omitting the lace trim and hanging loop. In addition, use only French knots for the small matryoshka's eyes. There is no pocket on the small doll. It may be necessary to change the zig-zag stitch width and length when working with the smaller appliqué pieces.

Oh, Dottie Tree

This simple yet adorable ornament is quick to make—perfect when you're in a crunch to make a handmade gift. Don't just stop at felted balls; you can decorate the tree with sequins or beads for a sparkly effect.

Designed and made by
Linda Lum DeBono

Finished size: 4½" x 7"

Materials

9" x 12" piece of green wool felt

Scrap of brown wool felt

8 assorted ⅜"-diameter felted balls

Assorted blue and green seed beads

Beading thread

Beading needle

Polyester fiberfill

Cutting

Patterns for the tree are on page 60.

From the green wool felt, cut:
   1 using tree pattern
   1 reversed using tree pattern

From the brown wool felt, cut:
   1 using trunk pattern
   1 reversed using trunk pattern

Directions

1 Place the tree trunk pieces wrong sides together and sew the side and bottom edges with matching thread and a zigzag stitch that's 3 mm wide and 2 mm long, leaving the top edge open. Position the stitch to overcast the felt edges.

2 Center the tree trunk along the bottom edge of the tree back's wrong side. The trunk should overlap the tree by ¼". Pin in place. Position the tree front on the tree back with wrong sides together, matching the raw edges, and pin. The upper edge of the tree trunk will be between the tree pieces.

3 Using green thread and the zigzag stitch from step 1, sew all around the tree. Begin by sewing across the top of the trunk, securing it to the tree. Leave an opening between the last corner and the trunk and lightly stuff the tree with polyester fiberfill (see "Stuffing Tips" on page 77). Finish sewing the tree edges to close the opening.

4 Hand sew the eight felted balls randomly across the front of the tree.

5 Thread a beading needle with a double strand of beading thread. Attach the thread securely to the top point of the tree with several small backstitches, hiding the thread tails between the felt layers. String enough beads to make a 7" length. Fasten off the thread with several small stitches through the top of the tree to make a hanging loop.

Petrie's Modern Polygon Hexagons Pillow

This is a nod to my university calculus days. Modern polygon hexagons are named after John Flinders Petrie, but I don't think he ever imagined them in holiday prints like this! I adore hexagons and I love them in any size. Large hexagons add drama because you can use cool novelty fabrics and mix them all up. The turquoise fabric on the ends of the pillow grounds the busyness of the prints with a wonderful splash of unusual color.

Designed and made by
Linda Lum DeBono

Finished size: 26" x 14"

Materials

Yardage is based on 42"-wide fabric unless otherwise specified.

7 squares, 10" x 10", of assorted holiday prints for the hexagons

Fat quarter of turquoise print for the side panels

½ yard of fabric for backing

28" x 17" rectangle of batting

Polyester fiberfill

Cutting

The hexagon pattern is on page 50.

From assorted holiday prints, cut:
 22 using hexagon pattern

From the turquoise print, cut:
 2 rectangles, 6½" x 14½"

From the backing fabric, cut:
 1 rectangle, 14½" x 26½"

Cutting Directional Prints

When cutting hexagons for the pillow front, position any directional prints to run between two sides, not two corners. The top of the design will be upright in the finished pillow, with the flat hexagon sides running horizontally.

Directions

Seam allowances are ¼" unless otherwise indicated.

1 Arrange the hexagons on a flat surface or design wall as shown. Sew the hexagons together in vertical columns, sewing only between the seamline intersections and backstitching at each end of the seam. There are three columns with four hexagons in each and two columns with five hexagons.

Travel Worthy

With their small size and Y seams, hexagons are a great project to piece by hand. Tuck them into a small plastic bag along with needle and thread for a portable project that's easy to tote.

Sew between points and backstitch at each end.

Make 3.

Make 2.

Good Point

Use a small punch or large needle to make a hole at each corner of the hexagon template, where the seamlines intersect. Transfer the locations to the wrong side of each fabric hexagon, and use the marks as a guide for starting and stopping seams.

4 Sew a turquoise rectangle to each side of the hexagon center.

5 Center the pieced pillow top right side up on the batting rectangle. Quilt by stitching ⅛" on each side of every seam within the hexagon panel. Mark vertical lines on the side panels 2¼" and 4½" from the seamlines and quilt along each line. Trim the batting to match the pillow top.

6 With right sides together, sew the pillow front to the pillow back, leaving a 5" opening for turning along the bottom edge.

7 Clip the corners diagonally to reduce bulk and turn the pillow right side out. Use a point turner or other tool to work the corners into place.

8 Stuff the pillow with polyester fiberfill. Fold the seam allowances to the wrong side along the opening and slip-stitch the opening closed.

2 Sew the columns of hexagons together using the Y-seam technique on page 51.

3 Press the pieced hexagons and trim the unit to measure 14½" square.

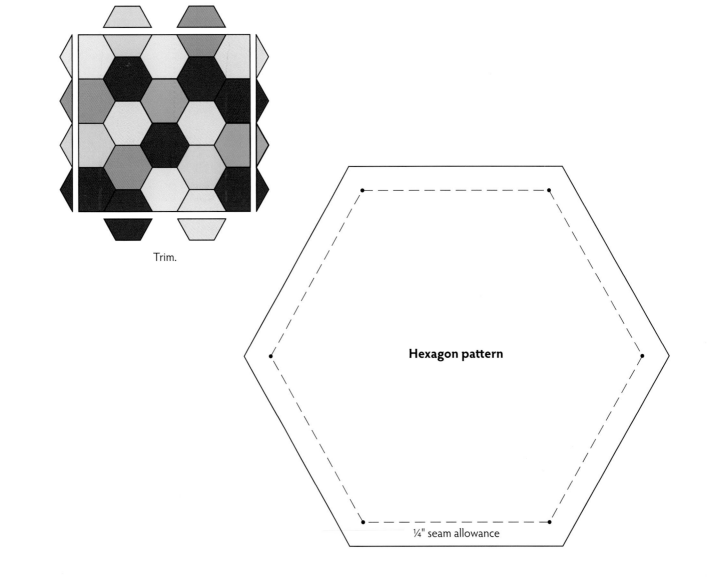

Trim.

Hexagon pattern

¼" seam allowance

Y Seams

The most important step to remember when sewing Y seams (or set-in seams) is to stitch only between the seamline intersections, leaving the seam allowances free.

1. Join the hexagons into columns.
2. Place two adjacent columns together, offsetting the hexagon points. With right sides together, align the first pair of hexagon sides (A). Stitch from one seamline intersection to the other, backstitching at each end of the seam.

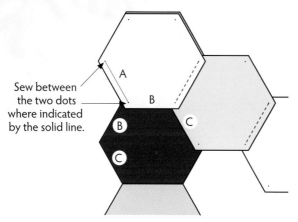

Sew between the two dots where indicated by the solid line.

3. Swing the top hexagon around to align its adjacent side with the corresponding hexagon side in the bottom column (B). Notice that, in the column underneath, the work has moved to a second hexagon. Sew the hexagon sides as before.

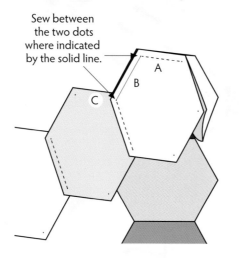

Sew between the two dots where indicated by the solid line.

4. Swing the top column around to align the first side of the next hexagon with the adjacent side of the hexagon in the column on the bottom and sew (C).
5. Repeat to join all the hexagons in the two columns, working with one side seam at a time. Do not sew across any seam allowances. Continue the process to join the remaining columns in the pillow top.

Be Merry Quilt

This is another take on the chevron pattern. A simple four-piece square, cleverly rotated, creates the lively zig-zags racing across the background of this merry little quilt.

Designed and made by
Linda Lum DeBono

Finished size: 35" x 55"
Block size: 5¾" x 5¾"

Materials

Yardage is based on 42"-wide fabric.

1¼ yards of white fabric for blocks

⅜ yard of light-blue tone-on-tone fabric for blocks

⅜ yard of light-blue candy-cane print for blocks

⅜ yard of green print for blocks

⅜ yard of red-striped fabric for appliqué background

¼ yard of red-dotted print for blocks

¼ yard of red snowflake print for blocks

¼ yard of lime-green print for appliqué

1½ yards of fabric for backing

½ yard of multicolored-striped fabric for the binding

40" x 59" piece of batting

9" x 12" piece of fusible web

22" x 8" tear-away stabilizer
  (see "Stabilizer" on page 75)

Template plastic

Cutting

Appliqué patterns are on page 63.

From the white fabric, cut:
  16 strips, 2½" x 40"

From the light-blue tone-on-tone fabric, cut:
  4 strips, 2½" x 40"

From the light-blue candy-cane print, cut:
  4 strips, 2½" x 40"

From the green print, cut:
  4 strips, 2½" x 40"

From the red-striped fabric, cut:
  1 rectangle, 9" x 33½"

From the red-dotted print, cut:
  2 strips, 2½" x 40"

From the red snowflake print, cut:
  2 strips, 2½" x 40"

From the multicolored-striped fabric, cut:
  5 strips, 2½" x 40"

Double-Strip Ruler

The Creative Grids 90° Double-Strip Ruler can be used to make quick work of the blocks for this project.

1. Cut the strips in the quantities listed in the cutting directions, but use the Double-Strip Ruler's gridded side as a guide to cut 2½"-wide strips. Assemble the strips in pairs as directed for traditional piecing.

2. With both the strip set and ruler right side up, align the bottom of the ruler triangles with the raw edge of the bottom strip. The dotted horizontal line on the ruler will align with the seam between the two strips.

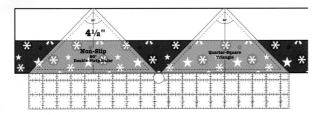

3. Cut along the triangle edges with a sharp rotary cutter. Both the tip-up and tip-down triangles will be used in the project.

For more information about the Double-Strip Ruler, see *Strip-Smart Quilts* (Martingale, 2011) by Kathy Brown.

Directions

Seam allowances are ¼" unless otherwise indicated.

1 Sew a white-print strip to each colored-print strip.

2 To make a template for cutting the triangles, draw a 6⅝" square on a piece of template plastic. Draw a diagonal line from corner to corner. Measure and mark a line 2¼" from and parallel to the center diagonal. Mark a second parallel line 2¼" above the first; it will just slice away the corner. Cut out the template shown by the shaded area.

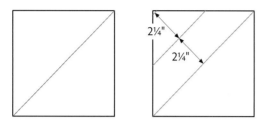

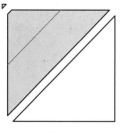

Trim.

3 Working with one strip set at a time, place the strip set on the cutting mat with the colored strip at the top. Align the 45° mark on a rotary cutting ruler with the seam between strips and trim the end of the strip set at an angle.

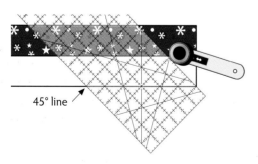

45° line

4 Rotate the strip set 180°. Position the template on the strip set, matching its edge to the diagonal line and its base to the top of the white strip. The line across the middle of the template should align with the strip-set seam. Trace the template edges and cut out the triangle.

Trace template and cut out triangles.

5 Continue cutting triangles that alternate pointing up and down along the length of the strip set; make four triangles with colored tips and three triangles with white tips.

6 Repeat with a second strip set containing the same color print, but this time begin step 3 with the colored strip on the bottom. After cutting two strip sets, you'll have seven triangles with white tips and seven with colored tips—14 triangles total. You may need to cut additional strip sets, or you may have a few triangles left over. Repeat as necessary to make the following groups of triangles, with an equal number of white and colored tips in each:

- White and light-blue tone-on-tone: make 24 total triangles (12 white and 12 blue tips)
- White and light-blue candy-cane print: make 24 total triangles (12 white and 12 blue tips)
- White and green print: make 24 total triangles (12 white and 12 green tips)
- White and red-dotted print: make 12 total triangles (six white and six red tips)
- White and red snowflake print: make 12 total triangles (six white and six red tips)

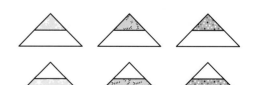

Make 12 of each.

Make 6 of each.

Don't Stretch

The edges of the triangles and squares in this quilt are all cut on the bias, so be careful not to stretch or distort the shapes when handling them. Applying spray starch to the fabric before cutting will help control the stretch.

7 Sew the pieced triangles together in pairs as shown to make a total of 48 blocks.

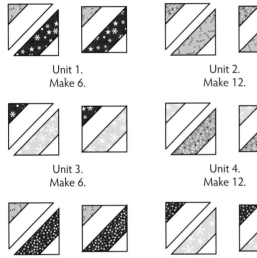

Unit 1.
Make 6.

Unit 2.
Make 12.

Unit 3.
Make 6.

Unit 4.
Make 12.

Unit 5.
Make 6.

Unit 6.
Make 6.

8 Trace the letters on page 63 onto fusible web. Be sure to trace two e and two r shapes. Following the manufacturer's instructions, iron the fusible web to the wrong side of the lime-green print and cut out the letters.

9 Appliqué the letters to the red-striped rectangle, referring to the illustration for placement. Place a layer of stabilizer underneath the fabric. Set the machine for a zigzag stitch that's 3 mm wide and 2 mm long. Using green thread, zigzag the letters to the background fabric, positioning the stitch to overcast the letter edges. Tear away the excess stabilizer.

Placement guide

10 Arrange the blocks as shown. Each row is made of six identical units, with alternate blocks rotated 90°. Notice the zigzags above the appliquéd band are oriented opposite those below.

11 Sew the blocks together in rows. Join the rows to make the quilt top, inserting the appliquéd band between block rows 2 and 3.

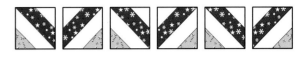

12 Layer the quilt top, batting, and backing to make a quilt sandwich. Baste the layers together. Stitch in the ditch along the zigzag seams to quilt, adding parallel rows of quilting stitches along the centers of the zigzag bands.

13 Remove the selvages from the striped binding strips and join them into one continuous length. Press the binding in half lengthwise with wrong sides together. Bind the edges of the quilt. See "Straight-Grain Binding" on page 77 for more information.

Holiday Musical Chairs Quilt

Remember playing the game musical chairs when we were little? I thought about that fun little game when I was designing this quilt. All of the blocks are made with 3" half-square triangles, plus one 6" square that's made from a fun fuchsia holiday print. This square moves around each block to find its home in each round. The fabric choices are yours and the fun is in making up your own blocks just by spinning the half-square triangles around.

Designed and made by
Linda Lum DeBono

Finished size: 40½" x 54½"
Block size: 12" x 12"

Materials

Yardage is based on 42"-wide fabric.

1 yard *total* of assorted white prints for blocks

½ yard of fuchsia print for focal squares

½ yard of green ornament print for blocks

⅜ yard of green tree print for blocks

⅜ yard of aqua print for blocks

⅜ yard of diamond print for blocks

½ yard of red-striped print for sashing

½ yard of black-and-white print for binding

1⅔ yards of fabric for backing

46" x 60" piece of batting

Optional: Thangles foundations for 3" finished
    half-square triangles

Fabric Choices

For each block in this quilt, you'll need one fuchsia square and 12 half-square triangles. You can mix and match the combinations of fabric used to make the 3" (finished) half-square triangles. Refer to the photograph and instructions to duplicate my choices, or feel free to make your own.

In general, each half-square triangle has one light and one medium or dark patch, although there are some pieced from two medium-value triangles. Three white print fabrics are used in the sample; their patterns are similar, so they're used interchangeably. The two green prints are similar values, so they're also easy to mix.

Cutting

If you prefer using Thangles foundation patterns to paper piece triangles, see "Using Thangles" on page 58 for optional cutting information.

From the assorted white prints, cut:
    50 squares, 3⅞" x 3⅞"; cut once diagonally to yield
        100 triangles

From the fuchsia print, cut:
    12 squares, 6½" x 6½"
    24 squares, 3⅞" x 3⅞"; cut once diagonally to yield
        48 triangles

From the green ornament print, cut:
    23 squares, 3⅞" x 3⅞"; cut once diagonally to yield
        46 triangles

From the green tree print, cut:
    16 squares, 3⅞" x 3⅞"; cut once diagonally to yield
        32 triangles

From the aqua print, cut:
    16 squares, 3⅞" x 3⅞"; cut once diagonally to yield
        32 triangles

From the diamond print, cut:
    16 squares, 3⅞" x 3⅞"; cut once diagonally to yield
    32 triangles

From the red-striped print, cut:
    8 rectangles, 2½" x 12½"
    3 strips, 2½" x 40½"

From the black-and-white print, cut:
    6 strips, 2½" x 40"

Directions

Seam allowances are ¼" unless otherwise indicated.

1. Join the triangles in pairs to make 144 half-square-triangle units as listed. You'll have extra triangles.

    • 33 green ornament and white units
    • 31 green tree and white units
    • 32 aqua and white units
    • 32 fuchsia and diamond units
    • 4 fuchsia and white units
    • 12 green ornament and fuchsia units

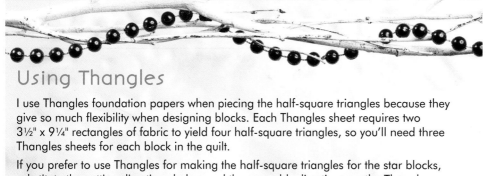

Using Thangles

I use Thangles foundation papers when piecing the half-square triangles because they give so much flexibility when designing blocks. Each Thangles sheet requires two 3½" x 9¼" rectangles of fabric to yield four half-square triangles, so you'll need three Thangles sheets for each block in the quilt.

If you prefer to use Thangles for making the half-square triangles for the star blocks, substitute the cutting directions below and the assembly directions on the Thangles package to make the units described in step 1. You'll have extra half-square-triangle units.

From the assorted white prints, cut:
26 rectangles, 3½" x 9¼"

From the fuchsia print, cut:
12 rectangles, 3½" x 9¼"

From the green ornament print, cut:
12 rectangles, 3½" x 9¼"

From the green tree print, cut:
8 rectangles, 3½" x 9¼"

From the aqua print, cut:
8 rectangles, 3½" x 9¼"

From the diamond print, cut:
8 rectangles, 3½" x 9¼"

2 Arrange the half-square-triangle units as shown to create 12 blocks, each four units wide and four units high. Use 12 half-square-triangle units and one 6½" fuchsia square in each block.

Block 1   Block 2   Block 3

Block 4   Block 5   Block 6

Block 7   Block 8   Block 9

Block 10   Block 11   Block 12

3 Sew each block together, combining the half-square triangles into rows or short columns to fit the fuchsia squares. Arrange the blocks into a quilt top that's three blocks wide and four blocks high.

4 Stitch three blocks together with two red-striped sashing rectangles to make a row. Repeat to make four rows.

5 Sew the four block rows together with the three red-striped sashing strips as shown.

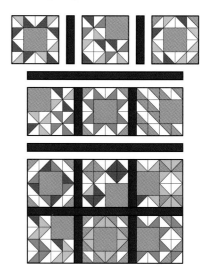

6 Layer the quilt top, batting, and backing. Quilt with an overall free-motion flame pattern.

7 Trim the backing and batting to match the quilt top. Remove the selvages from the black-and-white binding strips and join them to make a continuous length. Press the binding strip in half lengthwise with wrong sides together and bind the quilt edges. (See "Straight-Grain Binding" on page 77).

Patterns

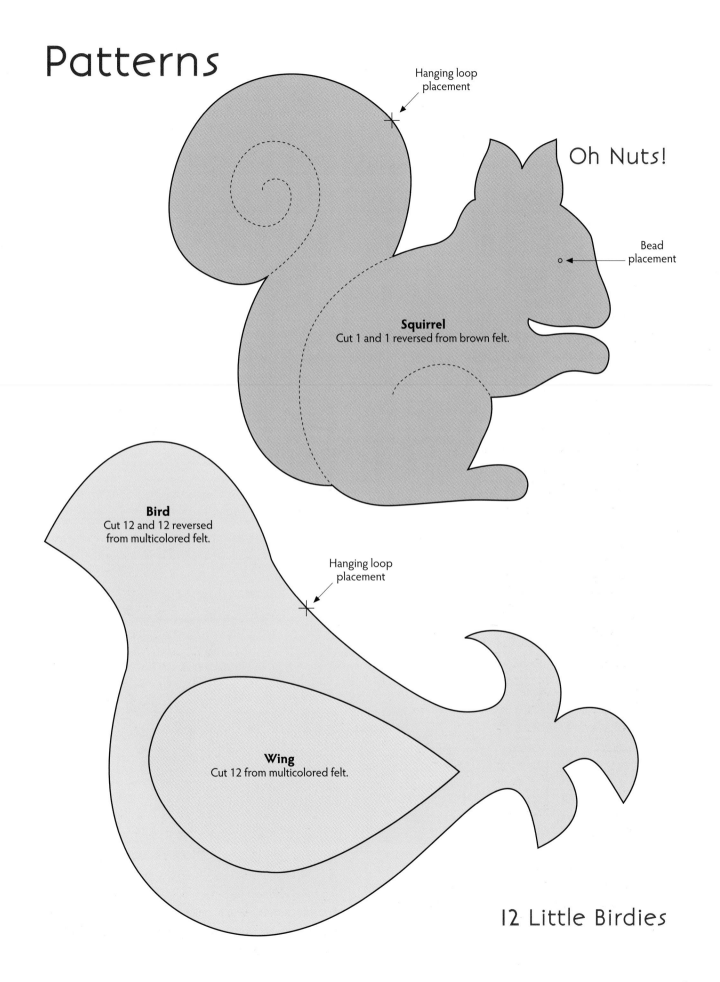

Hanging loop
placement

Oh Nuts!

Bead
placement

Squirrel
Cut 1 and 1 reversed from brown felt.

Bird
Cut 12 and 12 reversed
from multicolored felt.

Hanging loop
placement

Wing
Cut 12 from multicolored felt.

12 Little Birdies

Matryoshka Love

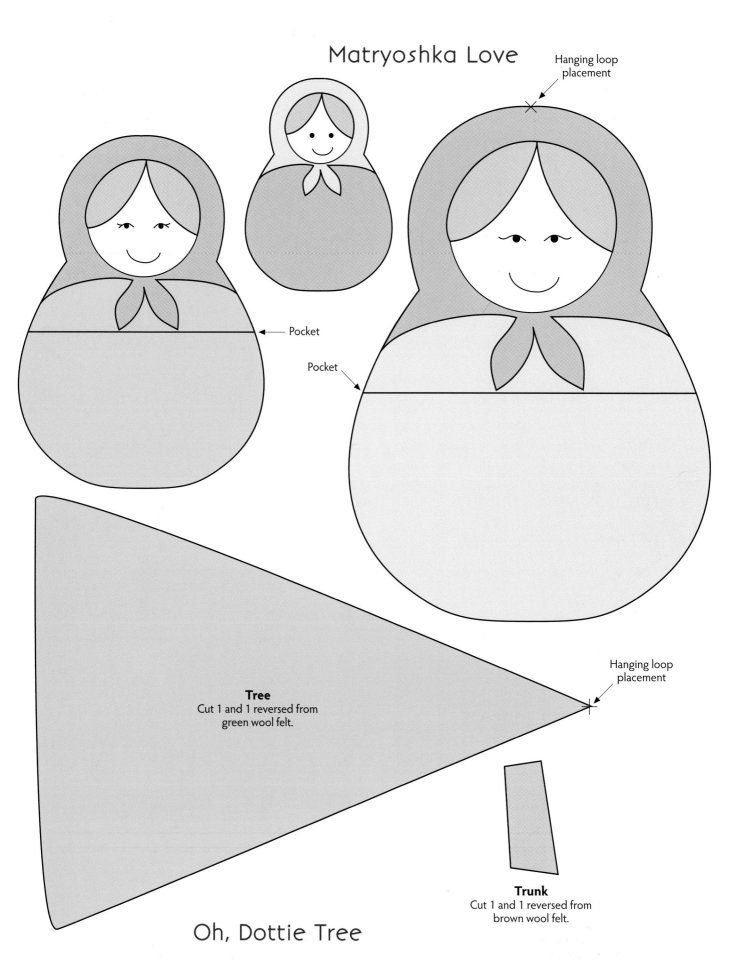

Hanging loop placement

Pocket

Pocket

Hanging loop placement

Tree
Cut 1 and 1 reversed from
green wool felt.

Trunk
Cut 1 and 1 reversed from
brown wool felt.

Oh, Dottie Tree

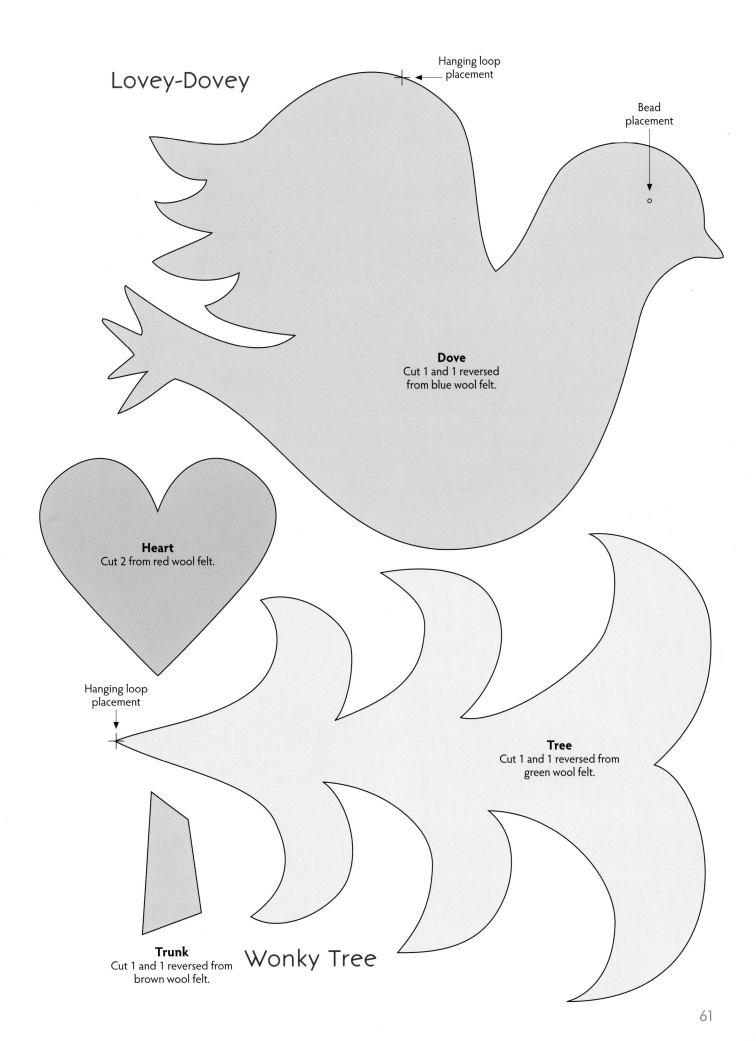

Lovey-Dovey

Hanging loop
placement

Bead
placement

Dove
Cut 1 and 1 reversed
from blue wool felt.

Heart
Cut 2 from red wool felt.

Hanging loop
placement

Tree
Cut 1 and 1 reversed from
green wool felt.

Trunk
Cut 1 and 1 reversed from
brown wool felt.

Wonky Tree

Noel Pillow

Patterns do not include seam allowances and are reversed for fusible appliqué.

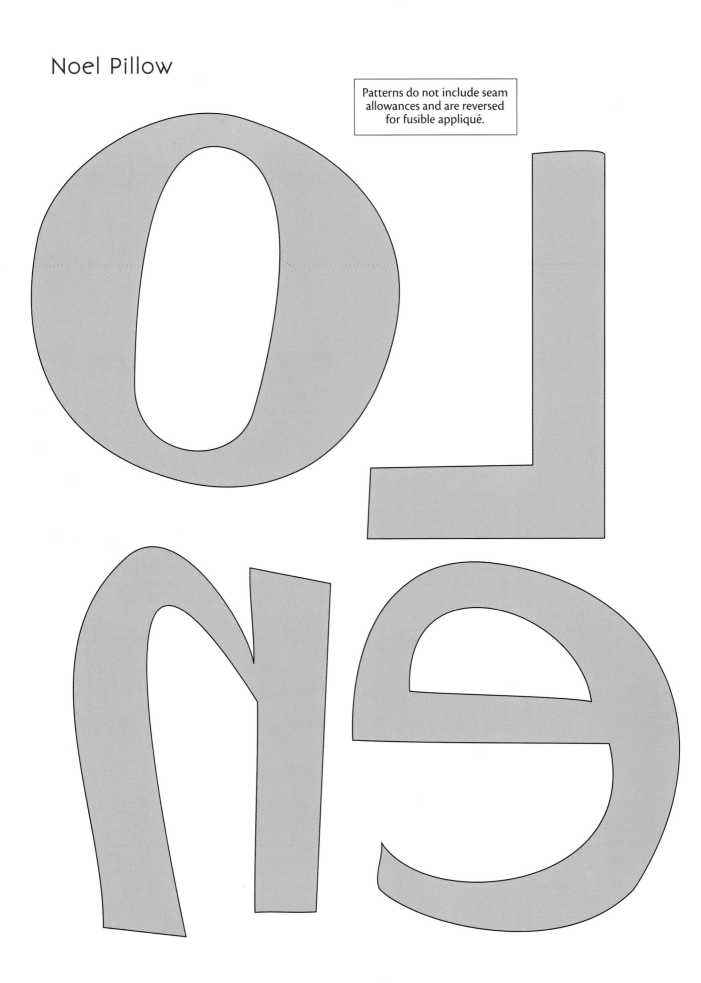

Be Merry Quilt

Patterns do not include seam allowances and are reversed for fusible appliqué.

Peace Place Mat

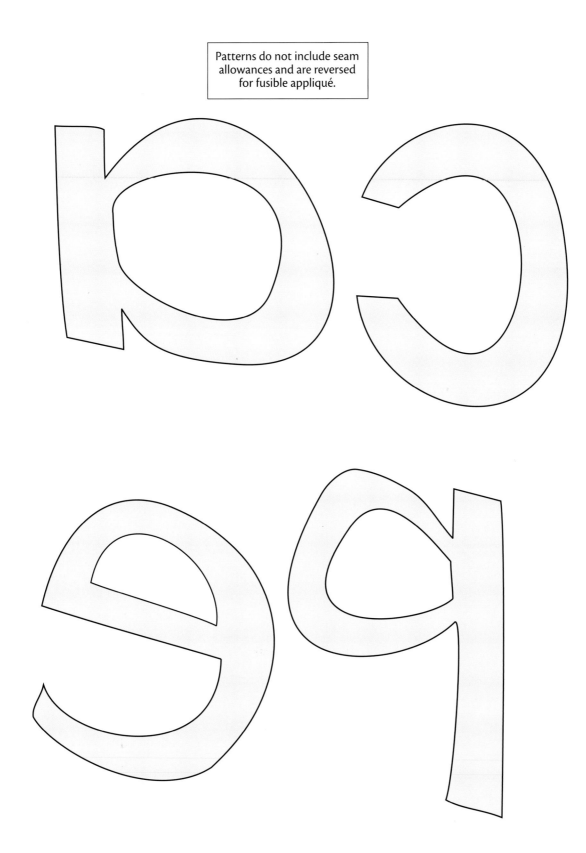

Patterns do not include seam allowances and are reversed for fusible appliqué.

Joy Place Mat

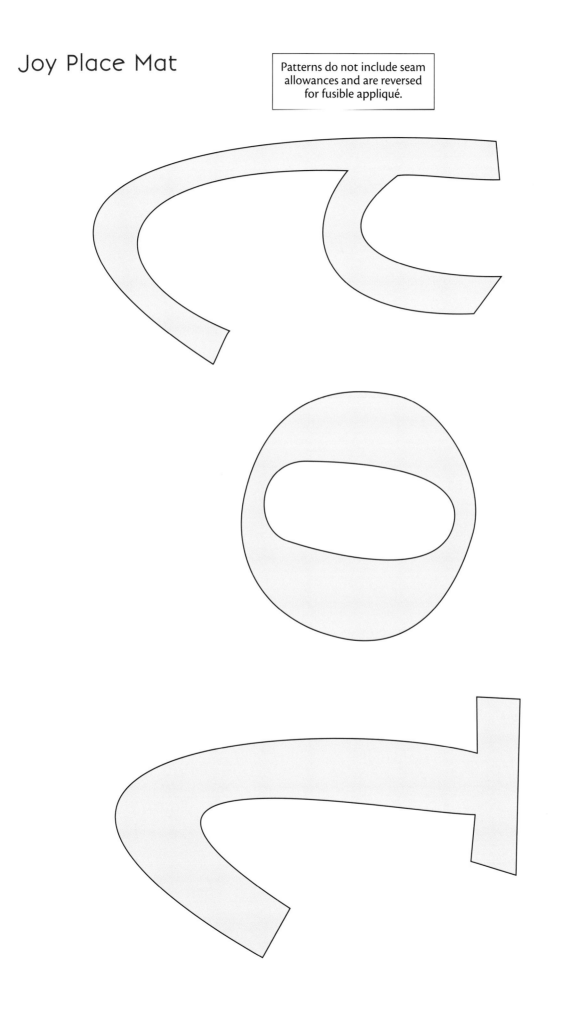

So Sweet
and
Rudolph's
Favorite
Stocking

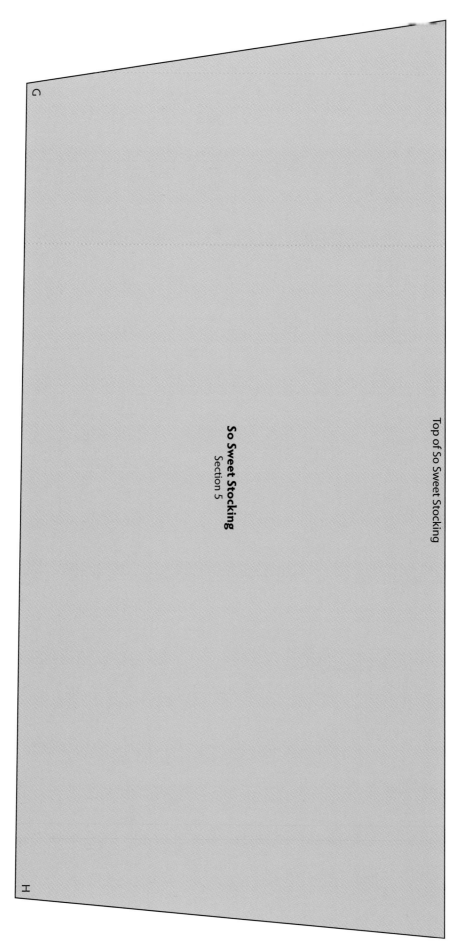

G

So Sweet Stocking
Section 5

Top of So Sweet Stocking

H

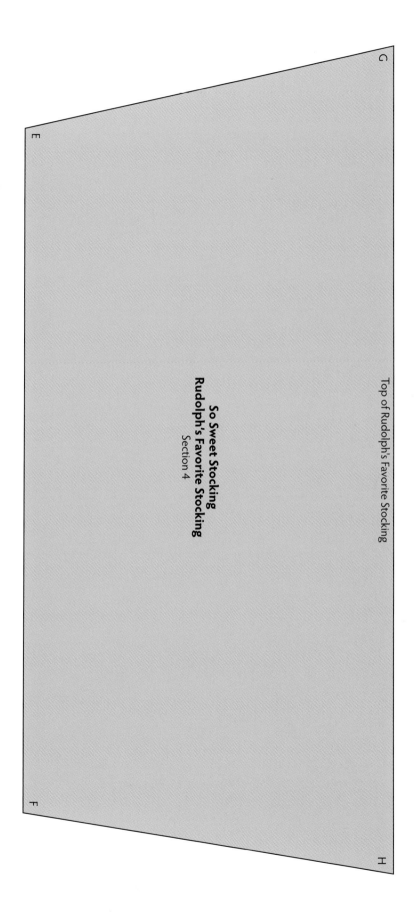

G

E

Top of Rudolph's Favorite Stocking

So Sweet Stocking
Rudolph's Favorite Stocking
Section 4

F

H

So Sweet Stocking
Rudolph's Favorite Stocking
Section 3

So Sweet Stocking
Rudolph's Favorite Stocking
Section 2

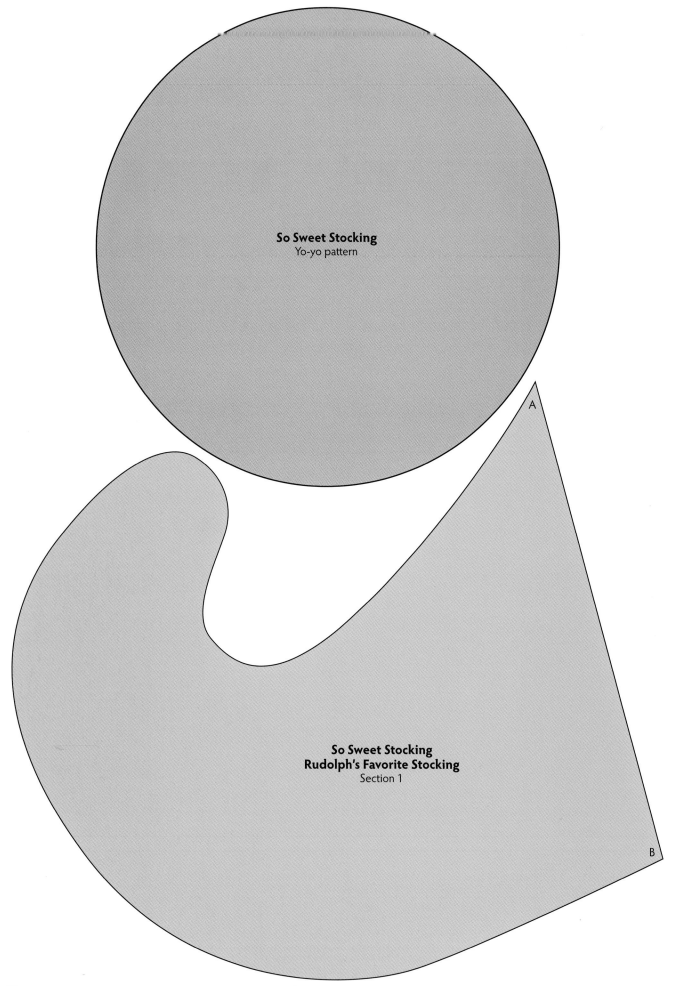

So Sweet Stocking
Yo-yo pattern

A

**So Sweet Stocking
Rudolph's Favorite Stocking**
Section 1

B

Rickrack Rainbow Stocking

A

B

Rickrack Rainbow Stocking
Section 1

Rickrack Rainbow Stocking
Section 2

C

D

A

B

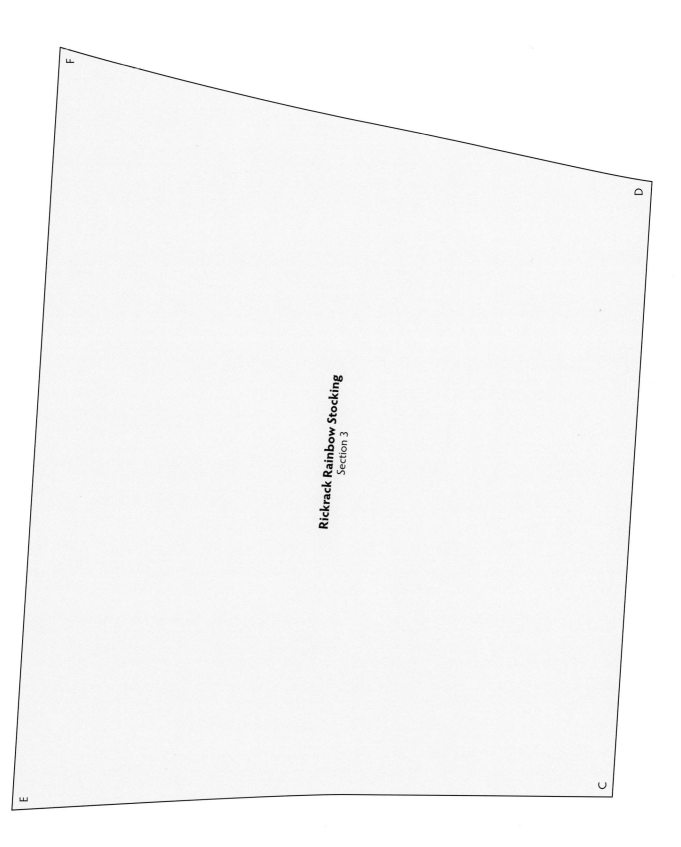

Rickrack Rainbow Stocking
Section 3

F

E

D

C

E

Rickrack Rainbow Stocking
Section 4

Top of stocking

F

Quilting and Sewing Basics

Basic skills are like a box of notions: it's important to have them handy whenever you're working on a project. Here are some essential techniques and product information useful for creating the projects in *Sew Merry and Bright*.

Selecting Fabrics

I used high-quality, 100% cotton, quilting-weight fabric for these designs. Yardage for these projects is based on purchased fabric described on the bolt as anywhere from 42" to 45" wide, with about 40" usable width after washing the fabric and trimming the selvages. (These are general guidelines; variations will occur from fabric to fabric.)

The term "fat quarter" is used in some materials lists to designate a precut length of fabric made by cutting a ½-yard of quilting cotton in half lengthwise. Fat quarters measure about 18" x 20", making them wider than a regular ¼-yard cut.

Selecting Felt

Some of the projects are made from felt. In addition to the craft felt readily available in fabric and variety stores, we now have choices containing various percentages of wool fiber. Here are the important terms to know:

Craft felt. A nonwoven, nonraveling fabric made from synthetic fibers. Craft felt is sold by the yard in 36" and 72" widths, as well as in "craft cuts" that measure about 9" x 12". Craft felt is usually the least expensive option, but its quality can vary widely, so be sure you choose a good-quality fabric.

Wool felt. A nonwoven, non-raveling fabric similar to craft felt, but containing a percentage of wool fiber. Many wool felts are blends of wool and rayon, but 100% wool felts are available. Wool felts tend to be heavier and more luxurious than craft felt, and were used for most of the projects in this book.

Felted wool. Woven or knitted wool fabrics that have been washed in hot water, causing shrinkage and "fulling." Felted wool is less likely to ravel than woolens that haven't been fulled, but some fraying can occur. The knit or woven structure of the original wool fabric may still be visible in felted wool.

Cutting Instructions

All rotary-cutting dimensions include ¼" seam allowances. Pattern pieces include ¼" seam allowances where required. All fabrics should be cut crosswise (from selvage to selvage) unless otherwise indicated.

Stabilizer

Sometimes adding a layer of tear-away stabilizer under the background fabric for machine appliqué makes all the difference in creating smooth stitches without ripples. When woven cotton appliqués are fused and lightly stitched to a stable woven background fabric, the fusible web acts as a stabilizer, and additional stabilizer may be unnecessary. However, when the appliqués are edged with satin zigzag stitches; the appliqué or background fabrics are knit, loosely woven, or unstable; or any other time a little extra help is desirable, a layer of tear-away stabilizer should be added.

Choose a nonwoven tear-away stabilizer from the machine-embroidery supplies available at stores and online. Stabilizers can be purchased with or without a temporary heat- or water-activated adhesive that provides even more support for the background fabric.

When the stitching is complete, carefully tear off the excess stabilizer, supporting the stitches with your fingers as you tear.

Fusible Machine Appliqué

1 Trace the appliqué image onto the paper side of the fusible web. Patterns are already reversed for tracing.

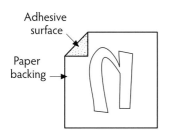

Adhesive surface

Paper backing

2 Roughly cut about ¼" outside the drawn lines. Place the adhesive side of the fusible web against the fabric wrong side and fuse in place, following manufacturer's instructions. If the fusible web has two release papers, remove the one without the traced outline before fusing.

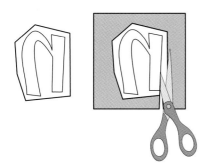

3 Cut out the image directly on the drawn line, cutting both the fusible web and the fabric. Remove the release paper, turn the appliqué shape fabric-side up, and fuse the fabric image to the right side of the appliqué background. Use a zigzag or blanket stitch to sew around the appliqué object.

Hand Stitches

Here are the hand stitches used in this book. Feel free to use different stitches from your repertoire for a more personalized effect.

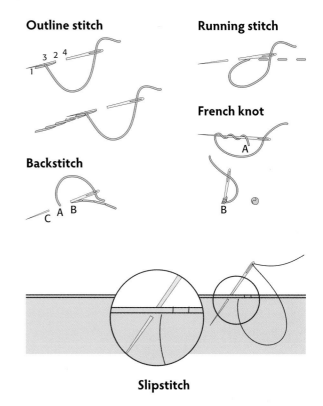

Outline stitch

Running stitch

Backstitch

French knot

Slipstitch

Making Yo-Yos

Yo-yos are gathered puffs of fabric experiencing renewed popularity. They are easy to make, portable, and well suited to scrappy projects. They can be displayed with either the gathered or flat surface revealed, and are often accented with a button or other embellishment.

1 Begin with a fabric circle twice the desired finished diameter of the yo-yo. Thread a needle with a double strand of strong thread and knot the end.

2 Fold ¼" of the circle's raw edge to the wrong side. Sew gathering stitches close to the folded edge. Work all the way around the circle and back to the beginning point.

3 Grasp the knotted end and the needle thread and pull the gathers tightly. Knot the ends together to secure the gathers, hiding the thread tails inside the yo-yo. Center the gathers on the yo-yo and finger-press

around the outer edge; don't flatten the gathers by pressing too firmly.

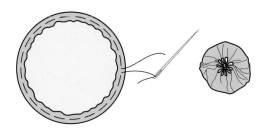

Think Big

It's counterintuitive, but longer running stitches will make a more tightly gathered yo-yo, with a smaller hole at the center. Keep your stitches, and the gaps between them, about ¼" long.

Stuffing Tips

There are several possibilities for stuffing small toys and ornaments. Some choose to use fabric or yarn scraps. Wool fibers are wonderful for stuffing pincushions because they keep needles shiny and rust free. For the projects in this book, however, polyester fiberfill is the stuffing of choice.

- Work with a small amount of stuffing at a time to keep the filling fluffy and free of clumps.
- Pull clumps of fiberfill apart with your fingers before inserting them into the project to help distribute the stuffing evenly.
- If the opening for stuffing is small, use a chopstick, knitting needle, or stuffing fork as an aid in stuffing the project's nooks and crannies.
- Begin stuffing with small areas far from the opening; work toward the opening as you stuff.

Quilting

Quilting—the stitches that hold the quilt top, batting, and backing together—can be as simple or as complex as you like. For the simplest quilting I stitch in the ditch, but for fancier designs I like to free-motion quilt. Each quilted project includes information about the pattern used for quilting stitches.

To stitch in the ditch, simply sew in the channels created by seams between patches. The quilting stitches sink into the layers, becoming invisible on the quilt top. A similar technique, outline quilting, involves sewing ⅛" to ¼" from the seams in the quilt top, outlining some or all of the patches.

For free-motion quilting, drop or cover the sewing machine's feed dogs and attach a free-motion or darning foot. (Check your machine's manual for specifics.) Some machines may also require adjustments to the tension setting. With the feed dogs disengaged, use your hands to move the quilt sandwich under the needle in any direction—forward, backward, sideways, or even in circles.

Freedom in Motion

I prefer not to mark a quilting design or path for free-motion quilting. I wear a wonderful pair of quilting gloves that grip the quilt surface and help me guide the fabric under the needle.

Straight-Grain Binding

All of the bindings in the projects were sewn with a straight-grain binding, except the center of the tree skirt. To create a straight-grain binding:

1 Cut 2½" x 40" strips of binding fabric. Cut as many strips as necessary to encircle the project perimeter, plus 10" or more for miters and joins.

2 Remove the selvages from the binding strips and join them end to end with diagonal seams to reduce bulk. To do this, overlap two strips at right angles with right sides together, forming a square at the overlap. Sew diagonally across the square from corner to corner. Trim the seam, leaving a ¼" seam allowance beyond the stitches. Press the seam allowances open.

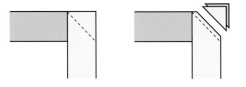

3 Press the assembled binding strip in half lengthwise with wrong sides together.

4 Begin pinning the binding to the quilt top near the center of the lower edge, matching the raw edges. Leave an 8" tail free at the beginning and begin sewing toward the first corner. Stop sewing ¼" from the corner and backstitch. Fold the binding as shown to miter the corner, pivot the quilt 90°, and sew the binding to the second side. Continue around the quilt, mitering each corner as you come to it.

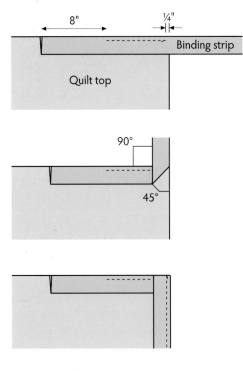

5 Stop sewing about 12" from the beginning edge of the binding and backstitch. Overlap the ends of the binding and trim the trailing edge so the overlap is 2½". Open the folded binding ends and sew the ends diagonally as shown. Trim, leaving a ¼" seam allowance, and press the seam open.

Overlap ends and trim to 2½".

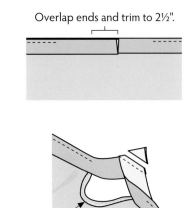

Unstitched quilt edge

6 Refold the binding strip and sew its remaining length to the quilt top.

7 Bring the folded edge of the binding to the quilt back, enclosing the raw edges. Slip-stitch the binding fold to the quilt back, mitering the corners.

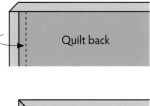

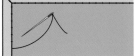

Acknowledgments

Mary Green, Karen Soltys, Cathy Reitan, Sheila Ryan, Paula Schlosser, Rebecca Kemp Brent, Shelly Garrison, Brent Kane, and the rest of the wonderful folks at Martingale. Thank you.

Karen Junquet and the Henry Glass family. Much appreciation.

Jennifer Keltner, Elizabeth Tisinger Beese, Jill Mead, Lisa Schumacher, and Meredith Corporation for continued support in all that I do.

Mark Lipinski. Thank you, my friend, for being you and for our friendship that's based on saying the truth.

Jodie Davis. Thank you for your support.

Toby Preston and her staff at Kindred Quilts in Clinton, New Jersey. You rock!

Colleen Gregory and Joanne Berson. Wonderful friends who happen to sew! Colleen, special thanks for the favor that you did for me.

Alex Veronelli, Elena Gregotti, and the amazing Aurifil family. Thank you for the gorgeous thread.

Mary Beth Hayes of Thangles. Great product!

My Facebook and Twitter friends. I thank you for being my friends!

Thank you to the following companies for supplying me and the rest of the quilting world with the most fabulous fabrics:

Henry Glass and Company (www.henryglassfabrics.com).
Robert Kaufman Fabrics (www.robertkaufman.com). Thanks, Kyle Sanchez.
Michael Miller Fabrics (www.michaelmillerfabrics.com). Thanks, Michael Steiner and Christine Osmers.
Moda Fabrics (www.unitednotions.com). Thanks, Lissa Collins Alexander.
Adornit (www.adornit.com). Thanks, Carolee Petersen McMullin and Georgana Hall.

Most of all, a big thank-you and much love to my family. My little elves, Adam and Alex, you are my inspiration. Reno, thank you for reading and providing insightful comments (even though this is payback for making me read something you wrote called "Analytical Applications of Surface Plasmon Resonance." I think this is a much more pleasant read, though).

Mom, I love you for loving my boys so much.

About the Author

Linda Lum DeBono

Color rocks Linda's world.

Linda first gained notoriety as a designer of bright and funky quilts. Along the way, she has shown her diverse talents by authoring books on knitting and scrapbooking and by exploring other color ranges as well. The phenomenal use of color and texture in her work is what makes her designs so special.

After graduating from the University of Toronto and working in the pharmaceutical industry for a few years, Linda and her husband moved to New Jersey for his job. Linda then taught herself how to sew and soon after she designed her first pattern, "Believe." She showed her patterns at her first Quilt Market when she was six months pregnant and it has been one awesome ride!

Since debuting her patterns to the world, she has designed fabric for Henry Glass in New York City. She has authored several books for Martingale and others. Her work has been seen in the wonderful pages of *American Patchwork & Quilting*, *Quilts and More*, and *Christmas 365*. Linda also teaches online for CraftEdu.